ENRICO FERMI
ATOMIC PIONEER

ENRICO FERMI
ATOMIC PIONEER

BY DORIS FABER

ILLUSTRATED BY DAVID HODGES

PRENTICE-HALL, INC.
ENGLEWOOD CLIFFS, N.J.

OTHER P-H BOOKS BY DORIS FABER:

CLARENCE DARROW:
Defender of the People

HORACE GREELEY:
The People's Editor

THE LIFE OF POCAHONTAS

ROBERT FROST:
America's Poet

Second printing........December, 1966

Enrico Fermi: Atomic Pioneer, by Doris Faber
© 1966 by Doris Faber

Library of Congress Catalog Card Number: 66–10563

Printed in the United States of America.

J 28307

Prentice-Hall International, Inc., *London*
Prentice-Hall of Australia, Pty., Ltd., *Sydney*
Prentice-Hall of Canada, Ltd., *Toronto*
Prentice-Hall of India (Private) Ltd., *New Delhi*
Prentice-Hall of Japan, Inc., *Tokyo*

ACKNOWLEDGMENT

I am most grateful to the University of Chicago Press for permission to tell some of the stories Mrs. Laura Fermi first told about her husband in her delightful *Atoms in the Family*. In addition, I must thank Dr. Herbert Anderson and various other people at the University of Chicago for so kindly providing additional material; and Mrs. Milton Weiner, who was Nella Fermi, for adding a few warm memories of her father. I would also like to thank Walter Sullivan, science editor of *The New York Times*, for reading what follows, but any errors that may have crept in are, of course, my own responsibility.

D.F.

CONTENTS

1

"EXCEPTIONAL!"

It was actually snowing. Twelve-year-old Enrico Fermi saw the flakes through his school window, and wished hard for a storm. But no such luck! Elsewhere in Italy, snow would be frosting mountain peaks; here in Rome, it melted as it touched the famous old stone buildings and busy streets. Still, the air was cold enough on this December afternoon in 1913, so that Enrico could try an experiment when he got home.

The Fermi family lived in an apartment house which looked quite grand, with marble statues in its garden. The apartments were far from grand, though, and lacked many comforts—including any form of heating.

It was so chilly in the dining room where Enrico and his brother sat down to do their homework together that their breath made little clouds as they talked. "But I have an idea," Enrico said.

Giulio, who was a year older than Enrico, waited with interest.

"Now watch closely," Enrico commanded. He made a pile of books in front of him, keeping one apart from the rest, and this he propped up against the pile so that he could read it from where he sat, without supporting it with his hands. "It is the hands that are most affected by the cold," he remarked.

"So?" Giulio demanded. "I am not yet impressed."

"So I will proceed as follows," said Enrico, with a wise smile. He bounced up and sat on his hands, which would surely keep them warm, then leaned forward and started to study his Latin grammar.

"Very fine," said Giulio. "But what will happen when you must turn the page?"

In reply, Enrico leaned farther forward and turned to the next page—with his tongue!

Fortunately, the climate of Rome was ordinarily milder, so Enrico did not find it necessary to repeat this experiment very often. But he and Giulio did many other sorts of experiments to-

2

In reply, Enrico leaned farther forward and turned to the next page—with his tongue!

gether. Only ten years earlier, in 1903, another pair of brothers—the Wright brothers—had showed off their first flying machine in distant America. Now, a decade later, the young Fermi brothers designed, built and tested their own model airplane engines.

"It is incredible that this is the work of children!" some people said.

How much more astonished these people would have been if they had known what else Enrico was doing. For instance, he had picked up a *geometry* book somewhere, and had already taught himself this branch of mathematics.

Indeed, whatever he read, he seemed to remember almost word for word. He could recite whole pages of poetry by heart. But other subjects were more interesting than poetry, he thought.

Why did a top spin?

Why did the strings of a violin make different sounds?

How did water really differ from solid materials?

These were the kinds of questions that fascinated him. At home, he and Giulio constantly tried experiments that might lead them toward the answers. They certainly appeared to have surprisingly active minds.

But some people who knew the Fermi family history were not too surprised. For the boys' grandfather had started life as a poor farmer, and then worked his way up to managing a duke's estate. Their own father had climbed still higher—he was a railway official, and had married a schoolteacher. Energy and brains surely seemed to run in this family.

Enrico, born on September 29, 1901, was the youngest of three children. He and Giulio had an older sister, Maria. All three Fermi children did unusually well in school. It even looked as if they might be able to go on to college. Except for the very rich, this was rare in Italy then; but these three might win scholarships.

The thing that was most unusual about the Fermi brothers, though, was the way they stayed so close to each other. They went hiking together, they studied together, they played tricks on Maria together—until tragedy struck.

When Enrico was fourteen, Giulio's throat became very sore. Then the doctor said he ought to go to the hospital for a simple operation. "Do not worry," the doctor told Mrs. Fermi. "The boy is in no danger." But the trouble was far more serious than anybody had thought . . . and Giulio died.

Being a boy, Enrico could not express his grief by weeping bitterly, as his mother and Maria did. Instead he tried to ease his sorrow—with books. He plunged into studying with a fierce energy.

He had no money to buy the new books he would have liked, yet that did not stop him. In an open-air market, among junk of all sorts, he found old books he could afford. He even found science books, and one afternoon he brought home a real prize—*Elementary Mathematical Physics.*

"You've no idea how interesting it is!" he told Maria after reading a few pages. "I'm learning about light waves." There was a long silence, while he read on. "It's wonderful!" he spoke up again. "It explains the motions of the planets!"

There was a still longer pause. "Do you know," Enrico broke out next, "it's written in Latin, and not Italian. I hadn't noticed."

Maria might have been astonished—if she had not already decided that her brother was probably a genius. He was short and stocky, and untidy about combing his mop of black hair, but what a brain he had! As the months went by, somebody else came to the same conclusion.

Because Enrico was also a healthy boy who craved exercise after so much reading, he got into the habit of walking to meet his father every evening. Although Mr. Fermi had missed going to college himself, he had a friend with much learning who often joined them. One evening,

Enrico calmly asked this man a question that had been bothering him.

"Is it true," he asked, *"that there is a branch of geometry in which important geometric properties are found without making use of the notion of measure?"*

The man looked startled. That was quite a question from a boy of his age! Mr. Fermi had said that his boy did well in school, but even so. . . .

"Yes, that's true," the man said gravely. "Such geometry is known as 'Projective Geometry.' I have a book that explains it, and the first chapter is not too difficult. Would you like to borrow it?"

Enrico nodded eagerly.

Several weeks later, Enrico returned the book, having read every page and solved all of the problems in the final section. As he handed it back, he mentioned that he had found solving the problems the most interesting part.

"What?" Now the man was really startled. He himself had never been able to solve some of the problems. There were more than *two hundred* of them in that final section, and it should take months, or even years, to solve them all. But perhaps the boy was exaggerating a bit; he would test him.

Enrico passed the test so easily that the man had no more doubts. "Mr. Fermi," he said, "your son is *exceptional!*"

2

A PALACE AND PADLOCKS

With no difficulty at all, Enrico finished a four-year high school course in three years. At the same time, he went through book after book that his father's friend loaned to him—and these were not simple books.

Because he was still fascinated by tops, he studied *theoretical mechanics,* the branch of science that explains the behavior of objects in motion. He also taught himself German, since many advanced scientific books were written in that language. Now there was no longer any question about whether he would go to college; obviously, he could win a scholarship.

But where should he go?

9

To the University of Pisa, his father's friend said firmly. And Enrico agreed. This famous old Italian university had a special program for promising science students, and by now he was sure he wanted to devote his life to physics. Yet his parents protested.

"We lost Giulio," Mrs. Fermi said sadly. "Now We must allow Enrico to leave us for four years? There is an excellent university here in Rome. . . ."

Gently, Enrico managed to convince his mother, and at last she gave her consent. At the age of seventeen, he went to Pisa to take a test. He got the highest mark ever recorded!

In Pisa, Enrico was assigned a tiny room of his own—in a palace. This beautiful old building where princes once had lived now belonged to the university.

It happened that Enrico started his advanced studies during a month that has gone down in history. November of 1918, the month he moved into the palace, was the month which saw the end of the First World War. Italy was on the winning side in the war, and the atmosphere throughout the country was festive. This just added to his excitement. He woke up every morning feeling like singing; he made friends easily. Everything about his new life in Pisa pleased him.

10

Even the one outstanding disadvantage to living in a stone palace that was more than three hundred years old failed to disturb him: In his little room in Pisa, it was cold, far colder than he had ever been in Rome. But thanks to his *scaldino*, Enrico did not have to rely on his tongue to turn pages while he was studying.

The *scaldino* was a small, long-handled pot filled with red-hot charcoal. With this on his lap, he could warm his stomach and his hands while he was reading.

Now he read more widely than ever, about physics and mathematics. Even more importantly, a laboratory was now available, where he could begin serious experiments of his own.

The very air of Pisa excited Enrico to try new sorts of experiments. For although it was an old city, filled with reminders of the past, the past here was rich in science history. From the top of the famed Leaning Tower that Enrico saw every day, Galileo himself was said to have dropped objects of different weights—to prove his theory that all falling bodies obey the same rules. Known everywhere as the great astronomer and mathematician and physicist who had laid the foundation for much of modern science, Galileo had been a student and then a professor at the University of Pisa late in the 1500s. Now, three and a half centuries later, possibly in the same building, Enrico Fermi started to experiment with X rays!

He had time for trying whatever interested him, because he did not have to keep up with his fellow students. *He was already so far ahead of them* that he could miss lectures almost whenever he chose.

But he certainly did not spend endless hours concentrating by himself in a laboratory or in his own room. He also found many other ways to make his college days race by delightfully. Most of these grew out of his membership in a select secret club which he and some of his friends had formed.

They named it "The Anti-Neighbor Society," and its only purpose was to pester other people. Since several of the members were very quick thinkers, they thought up some surprising ways to accomplish their mission—but none was more successful than their padlock plan.

This plan called for each member to carry a small padlock in his pocket, preferably painted a bright red or yellow. The plan worked best if the club members set out in teams of two. Then, while one of them stopped a fellow student to chat about the weather or some equally innocent topic, the other took the lock out of his pocket, deftly slipped the hasp through two opposite buttonholes of the victim's coat or jacket—and snapped it shut!

With a little practice, Fermi got to be such an expert at sneaking out his lock that he even trapped fellow members. Friend or foe, it took much anxious pleading before the key to free a victim was forthcoming.

In addition, the Anti-Neighbors also perfected a system for settling a pan of water on top of a door—in such a way that the next person passing through the doorway would be sure of a shower. They even went so far as to manufacture a terrible-smelling bomb, which they exploded in a lecture room. *That* seemed going too far to college authorities: several members, Fermi among them, were almost expelled.

Only a plea for mercy, by a professor who said that high spirits should be pardoned in young men with such good minds, saved them from having to go home in disgrace.

Somewhat sobered then, the club members took to mountain-climbing instead. Every Sunday, Fermi and one or more of his friends put on hiking boots and went off on an expedition. Fermi's legs were short—he had reached his full height by now, not many inches above five feet— but still he could climb as fast and far as anybody else. He even kept up with his friend, Franco Rasetti, and that was no easy task.

For the tall, thin Rasetti was an expert on bugs of all kinds. He was studying physics because he already knew so much about his own

13

subject that he wanted the challenge of something new. But he could never resist racing to catch any unusual butterflies he saw as they climbed. So Fermi spent many a Sunday racing up and down mountainsides after his friend—and butterflies.

Yet despite his many outside interests, Fermi by no means neglected physics. During his last year in college, he even taught a course—to one of his professors. "You are such a clear thinker!" the professor told him. "I can always understand what you explain." So even before getting his college degree, Fermi stood at the blackboard in a physics lecture room day after day, explaining the Einstein theory of relativity to this professor.

A new era was opening up in physics as the result of the work of the great German scientist, Albert Einstein. A part of what he had discovered could be summed up comparatively simply. His theory said there must be enormous stores of *energy* locked up in the tiny particles which made up every substance on earth. Energy, to physicists, means *the capacity for performing work*. Coal, oil and falling water were common sources of energy.

To grasp the enormity of the hidden energy, it is necessary to know that *light* travels *186,000 miles a second*. Then multiply *186,000* times

. . . explaining the *Einstein theory of relativity* to this professor.

186,000—and the tremendous number that results is represented in science by the symbol c^2. Einstein said the *energy* locked in any substance must equal its *mass multiplied by c^2*.

$E = mc^2$ is the historic way he put it.

Thus, a single pound of any substance—if it could somehow be made to yield up its hidden energy—would release as much power as *five million pounds of coal* did in the process of ordinary burning.

There was a great deal more to Einstein's theory, but it took much skill in mathematics and in advanced physics to be able to understand it. At the age of twenty, Enrico Fermi had easily mastered it.

By now, he realized he had a mind that was quite remarkable. Without being conceited, he simply accepted this as a fact—the way he accepted the fact that he had gray eyes. So he cheerfully explained Einstein's theory to his professor.

Then in July of 1922, Fermi appeared before a panel of professors. He had completed all the work required for a Ph.D. degree in four years; it usually takes seven. All that remained before he was entitled to be called Dr. Fermi was an oral test. His professors asked him only a few questions, then awarded him his degree "with the highest honors."

3

PROFESSOR FERMI

That autumn, Fermi reached the age of twenty-one. He was in Rome then with his parents, wondering what to do next. He had no doubt that physics was the field for him—and ideas for new ways to explain some very complex problems kept popping into his mind. Yet he needed money to live on, and a laboratory.

A job teaching at a university would suit him best, but such posts almost never went to young men, no matter how brilliant they might be. Indeed, jobs of any kind were not easy to find.

For times were hard in Italy. Peace had not brought prosperity, and there was much discontent. Then, only three weeks after Fermi's birthday, came one of the great turning points of modern history. As Fermi sat talking about his own future with a physics professor, a horde of hoodlums changed the future of Europe.

They came marching through the gates of Rome, and took over the city quickly. These were rough characters wearing black shirts, and they called themselves *Fascists*. Their leader, an angry man named Mussolini, bragged *he* would make the trains run on time again; *he* would fix everything that was wrong in Italy.

Fermi had never been much interested in politics. But now he had to pay attention to what was happening right before his eyes—and he did not like what he saw. It seemed clear to him that, sooner or later, Mussolini would do away with all freedom in Italy.

"It means that young people like me will have to leave the country," Fermi told his sister.

Maria, already a public school teacher and quite content with things as they were, looked shocked. "Leave Italy? But where would you go?"

"Somewhere . . ." Fermi shrugged. "The world is large."

Within a few weeks, he did leave the country. But this trip, to Germany and Denmark, was only for the purpose of further study. After two winters abroad, where his expenses were paid

18

So he began to organize weekend hikes . . .

by a special fund set up to help outstanding students, he returned to Rome. There, at the age of twenty-three, he first heard himself called Professor Fermi.

This was at the University of Rome. But he really had the lower rank of instructor, so he was not entitled to the honor of being addressed as professor. Furthermore, he was teaching mathematics, not physics—much to his regret. Still, he found it pleasant to be part of the university community, and he bought himself a new suit to celebrate. He thought its yellowish-brown was quite a stylish shade. But soon, alas, the suit became too tight. He loved exercise, and decided he had to have more of it, to lose some weight.

So he began to organize weekend hikes in the countryside around Rome. One student who sometimes came along, a pretty girl named Laura Capon, interested Fermi. She liked to tease him—she even told him the suit he was so proud of was much too yellow for a dignified professor. Somehow, he never minded her teasing.

But pleasant as all this was, Fermi felt uneasy. Ideas for physics projects kept coming to him, and he was impatient to get to work on them. He thought that if a man was going to accomplish anything really important in physics, or any other branch of science, he had to do it while he was young, when his own energy was at its peak.

So he packed up at the end of the year and went to the city of Florence, where he had been appointed to a teaching post that would give him more time for his own work. This proved a wise move for many reasons. For here he had the opportunity he had craved. Here he produced his first major contribution to the world of science.

During this period, physicists in many countries were finding the answers to a variety of questions that had always baffled mankind. The ancient Greeks had suggested that every substance was made up of unbelievably small particles called *atoms*—and now all sorts of new facts about atoms were being discovered.

Why did the atoms in a *gas* behave differently from the atoms in a solid or a liquid substance? Fermi took this question as his own special challenge—and he found the answer, in the form of a complicated series of figures.

In the same way that a great poet suddenly finds just the word he wants, Fermi suddenly thought of a possible approach to the problem. And then because his mind was stocked with an enormous amount of scientific information, and because he was patient and careful and so expert at mathematics, he was able to work out a sort of chart to back up the idea that had come to him.

Then he wrote a report about his work, which was published in a magazine for scientists—and as a result, he was invited to return to Rome. At the age of twenty-six, he became a professor of physics at the great university there!

"Only one or two men like Fermi are born in a century," the head of the physics department told people who wondered why so young a man had been selected.

Naturally, Fermi was happy to be back in Rome. Now he had a position of more importance, and more opportunities for scientific research. And it seemed that Mussolini would not be so bad, after all; he seemed to be letting scientists alone.

But there were also many personal reasons why Fermi was pleased by the new turn his life had taken. Rome was his home, and his family lived there. Many good friends were there, too, as well as a certain pretty girl whom he had not seen in several years.

It happened, though, that not until he went away to the mountains for his summer vacation did he come across Laura Capon again. She was vacationing with her family in the same Alpine village he had chosen. So were a number of other young people who all enjoyed hiking.

When the whole group set out to go up or

down a sunny path, it somehow always came about that Fermi was walking beside Miss Capon. She had not forgot him, or lost her fondness for teasing him. Now he teased her a little, too. He told her he was thinking of doing something exciting when he got back to the city. He might buy a car, he said, or perhaps he might even find himself a wife. He would look for a blonde, he said, since yellow was his favorite color, and if he could not find a blonde he liked, he would buy a car instead. Miss Capon, who had lovely, wavy dark hair, did not seem to be able to think of any light-hearted answer this time. Indeed, she was rather silent for the rest of his stay.

On returning to the city, Fermi did buy a car —a tiny two-seater the color of egg yolks. He wrote and told Miss Capon about it, for she was still away. Only after she got back to Rome did she learn that Fermi had been teasing her all along. On July 19, 1928, they were married.

4

NO. 93?

On their honeymoon in the Alps, Fermi decided to try out one of his theories. A good teacher could teach anybody any subject, he thought. So he decided, one rainy afternoon, to start teaching his bride advanced physics.

Mrs. Fermi had studied science in college and was by no means a slow student. Indeed, she had a very good mind of her own, and she used it to defeat her husband. She let him lecture for a few minutes on the subject of the speed of light and the speed of electromagnetic waves. The speed of both could be expressed by the same number, he told her. "Therefore," he said, "light is nothing else but electromagnetic waves."

"How can you say so?" Mrs. Fermi demanded.

"We have just demonstrated it," Fermi said patiently.

"I don't think so," said Mrs. Fermi. "You proved only that through some mathematical steps you can obtain two equal numbers. But now you talk of the equality of two things. You can't do that!"

So Enrico Fermi had to give up. For she knew she could not possibly keep up with her husband when it came to physics—and thought the sooner he knew this, too, the happier they would be.

Even though Mrs. Fermi refused to learn physics, the years following their marriage were very happy. Still, it was a problem being married to a brilliant man, as Mrs. Fermi and the wife of Franco Rasetti, Fermi's old butterfly-hunting friend, both discovered. Now Rasetti was in Rome, too. He was part of the group of talented physicists forming around Fermi at the University of Rome. Almost every weekend, the two couples went to the country or the seashore, and as they walked along together, they played a game.

"What is the name of this shell?" Rasetti would ask his wife.

The poor woman could only sigh and murmur she did not know.

"Fantastic!" Rasetti would say. "You don't

recognize this common bivalve mollusk?"

Then it would be Mrs. Fermi's turn. "I want to be kind this time," Rasetti would say. "I'll ask you a really easy question. What is the capital of Afghanistan?"

While her husband grinned delightedly, Mrs. Fermi could only shake her head.

"Fantastic!" Rasetti would say. "You don't even know the name of the capital of a country 270,000 square miles in area?"

For his part, Fermi would whip out the slide rule he always carried in his pocket, and easily answer the question Rasetti asked him about the area of an ant's brain. Then he would ask a few stumpers of his own. At last, the two wives got so desperate that they studied the first volume of an encyclopedia all week—and when Sunday came, *they* had some questions ready. "What is the population of Alexandria in Egypt?" Mrs. Fermi sweetly asked her husband. For once, he was speechless.

All week long, Fermi worked very hard. He was up at five-thirty, sitting in his bathrobe at the large study table that served him as a desk. For exactly two hours, he jotted figures in the series of notebooks he kept, until suddenly, as if an alarm clock had rung, he jumped up to dress for breakfast. After a morning at the university, he was back home precisely at one o'clock. He and his wife had a leisurely lunch in their comfortable apartment. Then he read newspapers or played tennis until precisely three o'clock when he returned to the university. Supper was at eight, and bedtime at half-past nine.

Fermi's main interest during this period was in *theoretical physics.* Applying himself to various unexplained problems, he developed theories that seemed to explain them. Because he was making a name for himself, in the summer of 1930 he was invited to take part in a special meeting on theoretical physics thousands of miles from Rome, at the University of Michigan in the United States.

Then he had to test another of his theories that had nothing to do with physics. It seemed to him there was no trick to learning a new language: one merely picked out an entertaining book written in the language, got a dictionary, and sat down to read the book. After reading ten pages of *The Call of the Wild* by Jack London, Fermi put aside his dictionary, then proceeded on his own steam to finish the adventure story. He read about a dozen books this way, before sailing.

And his theory worked! At least he managed not too badly in Michigan—while his wife, who had studied English in school in Rome, could hardly understand a word she heard all summer.

Much about America seemed strange to them both, yet they immediately liked the warm, friendly Americans they met.

After this, Fermi made several summer trips to various American colleges, but his wife stayed home. In 1931, their daughter Nella was born; five years later, they had a son Giulio, named for Fermi's brother who had died. So Mrs. Fermi was too busy with the children to travel.

By meeting so many other physicists, and by reading the magazines where reports on new research were printed, Fermi kept in touch with new developments in his field. Gradually, he began to think of changing his own area of work. Instead of theoretical physics, he became more and more interested in *experimental* physics. In 1934, he decided to switch.

What made him change was an exciting discovery by a French physicist and his wife— Frédéric Joliot and Irene Curie Joliot. She was the daughter of the famed Marie and Pierre Curie, who had discovered the element *radium*. (In chemistry, an element is a substance which cannot be separated into any other substance by ordinary chemical means; only ninety-two elements were known to man.)

Madame Curie had pioneered in studying *radiation*, the process by which radium emits certain "rays," and also the general name given to the ray-like stream of particles that are re-mitted. After Madame Curie, various English and French scientists had found that radiation was composed of several kinds of "rays." And they had also proved that these "rays" came from certain atoms, like radium, as they *changed*. This, in itself, was a momentous discovery. If atoms *could change*, which many scientists had previously doubted, then it might actually be possible to get at the energy Einstein had said was locked in every atom. Now Madame Curie's daughter and son-in-law took the world a great step beyond any previous research.

In the language of science, radium and a few other elements were naturally *radioactive;* the way they gave off their ray-like streams was called *radioactivity.* What the Joliots did in 1934 was to produce *artificial radioactivity.*

They did this by bombarding common alumi-num with certain particles that were among those that radium gave off naturally. Then the whole world of science was excited to learn that the aluminum was transformed. It became a different substance—a form of phosphorous, which is an element with an atom similar to the radium atom. And this new phosphorous was radioactive!

To Fermi's mind, the news opened up all sorts of possibilities. The kind of particles the Joliots

This patient physicist went to every chemical supply company in Rome, and he came back with what Fermi wanted.

had used were, for various reasons, unsuitable for bombarding heavier atoms than that of aluminum. But it occurred to him that there might be a better sort of "ray gun" for bombarding other elements. He thought of using *neutrons* to see if he could change other elements. Neutrons had only recently been identified as particles that were part of the *nucleus,* or inner core, of atoms. They were difficult to get at with the scientific methods known in the 1930's, but Fermi worked out a system for getting a stream of neutrons to bombard the targets he selected.

Then he sent one of his fellow physicists out with a paper shopping bag and a shopping list. There were ninety-two items on the list—the ninety-two known elements. This patient physicist went to every chemical supply company in Rome, and he came back with what Fermi wanted. Now the experiments could start.

Fermi began by bombarding hydrogen, the lightest element, with his neutrons. Nothing happened. Nor did he achieve any better success with the next five elements he tried. But the sixth—*fluorine*—turned radioactive!

Methodically, Fermi continued down the whole list of elements, and with each one after fluorine he achieved interesting results. Every element he bombarded with neutrons became radioactive; each changed somewhat, usually to another element quite similar in atomic weight. Then, when he came to the heaviest element of all, the last one on his list—*uranium* . . . Fermi became a hero!

Neither he nor his aides could say what it was their uranium had changed into, but they thought that they might have produced an entirely new element, one that had never existed before on the earth. However, because they were not sure of this, they made no such claim.

But now politics changed Fermi's future. The head of the physics department at the University of Rome knew that it would please Mussolini if an Italian scientist made a great discovery. So the head of the physics department took matters into his own hands. *He* made a speech about Fermi's work—and the next day there was this headline across an ocean in *The New York Times:*

ITALIAN PRODUCES 93RD ELEMENT BY BOMBARDING URANIUM

5

GOLDFISH—AND A PRIZE!

Fermi was rather embarrassed by the publicity that now came his way. Had he but known it, he did indeed deserve much credit. But not for another few years would another team of scientists succeed in discovering exactly what he had accomplished.

Meanwhile, he and the talented men who had gathered around him were busy with more neutron experiments. They kept testing various metals—and they found something they had not bargained for.

It all started with one of those happy accidents that fill the history of science. When testing silver, some of Fermi's assistants happened to place a piece of the metal near the corner of the lead box in which the bombarding was being done, instead of in the middle of the box. Surprisingly, the radioactivity that was produced by this test differed a little from previous results.

Fermi was interested at once. He suggested putting a piece of silver right on a wooden table, then aiming the neutron "gun" at it. Again the results varied a little from any past trial. They moved the metal once more, and once more the results were different. It became a game to think of new ways to get a piece of silver to emit a different amount of radiation.

In each case, the results were similar, but not identical. Obviously, it *did* make a difference where the silver sat when it was being bombarded. Then Fermi had a new idea. He suggested setting a thin plate of lead between the silver and the tube that was his neutron "gun." By now, everybody in the physics department had stopped to watch the curious tests Fermi was making. And there were whistles of astonishment when it turned out that passing through a heavy substance like lead actually helped the neutrons: this time, the silver was slightly *more* radioactive than after previous tests.

"Let's try a light substance next," Fermi said. "For instance, *paraffin*."

So a hole was bored in a large block of paraffin, and the neutron tube was put inside it. Then this strange weapon was aimed at the silver. Other physicists crowded around Fermi as he held a Geiger counter over the silver. This is an instrument that measures radioactivity, by clicking faster and faster as radioactivity increases.

Held over that bar of silver, the Geiger counter click-clicked *a hundred times* faster than it had after any previous silver experiments.

Excited voices rose above the clicking.

"Fantastic!"

"Incredible!"

"It's black magic!"

But Fermi's face wore a thoughtful look. *Why* had this amazing increase occurred? While he sat eating his lunch, he worked out a possible answer.

Paraffin was rich in hydrogen, he reasoned, and hydrogen atoms were so arranged that they might *slow down* neutrons colliding with them. Thus it would be easier for silver atoms to capture these *slow neutrons.*

Then, if more silver atoms were able to catch a neutron, more silver atoms would change— and there was bound to be a spectacular increase in the radioactivity produced.

"It's like a ball game," he explained to his

wife. "Slow balls are caught much easier by ball players than fast balls are. So slow neutrons should have a much better chance than fast neutrons of being caught by silver atoms."

As soon as he returned to the university, Fermi set out to test his theory. If he was right, any substance containing a large amount of hydrogen would do what the paraffin had done. Ordinary water was two-thirds hydrogen. "Let's see what water does," he suggested.

But he wanted a large amount of water, and he wanted it quickly. How could he manage this? No sooner had he asked the question than he had the answer. The University of Rome's physics department was housed then in an old building that had once been a convent. Out in the back, there was a lovely old garden, with a fountain splashing into a pool where goldfish swam lazily.

Suddenly, a crowd of physicists, led by a short, smiling man, came striding along the path toward this pool. Fermi dropped his neutron "gun" in at one end, and the bar of silver at the other. While goldfish went on gracefully swimming, the men standing above them waited in tense silence. Then Fermi removed the silver to test it.

And the counter clicked so fast there could be

no doubt at all. The experiment had worked! Men shouted and slapped each other's backs. Enrico Fermi had found a great new tool for scientific research—*the slow neutron!*

But his triumph was clouded by political troubles. What Fermi had feared when Mussolini first came to power now was happening. In 1935, Mussolini embarked on an adventure that horrified much of the rest of the world. He declared war on the African kingdom of Ethiopia, and sent an army to conquer it. Shouting that Italy must regain its grandeur as the center of a great empire, he ordered the bombing of defenseless villages.

At first, Fermi and his wife were caught up with their fellow Italians in a surge of patriotic feeling. Like good Italian women all over the country, Mrs. Fermi gave her gold wedding ring to be melted down to pay for the supplies that Italy's army needed. But soon she and her husband were shaking their heads as they read the papers every day. Mussolini was raving like a madman! Now they began to talk seriously about leaving their native land—to live somewhere else.

But Mrs. Fermi kept hesitating at the idea. It was hard for her to think of starting life afresh in another country, far from many people and

39

places she loved. Fermi's parents had died by now, but she had a large family. She hesitated, until another turn in world events convinced her that she had no choice.

A few years earlier, Adolf Hitler, a far harsher dictator than Mussolini, had seized control in Germany. Although most of the civilized world was condemning Mussolini for his African adventure, Adolf Hitler, in Germany, fully approved. Now Hitler was Mussolini's only foreign friend, and Mussolini had to please him.

Hitler had organized camps in his own country, where men, women and children were being killed by the thousands. His goal was to wipe out everybody who had been born into the Jewish religion, and anybody who dared to oppose him.

Pushed by Hitler, Mussolini now began to announce new rules in Italy, restricting the lives of Italian Jews. Worse might soon be expected, and while Fermi himself was a Catholic, Mrs. Fermi had been born Jewish. But even if she and their children were not threatened, Fermi felt strongly that the new rules were disgraceful. Now he insisted that they had to start planning to leave Italy, and she could object no longer.

There was no question about where they would go. Several American universities had asked Fermi to come and teach their students, and do his research in their laboratories. But

Mussolini would not forbid a Nobel Prize winner to go to
Sweden, to accept his prize in person.

how would they get to America? For no Italian could leave Italy, even on a vacation, unless the government approved of the trip. And passports for Mrs. Fermi and the children would be very hard to get.

Then, early on the morning of November 10, 1938, the telephone rang in the Fermis' apartment—and the problem was solved!

The call might have seemed mysterious. On the other end of the line, an operator said: "Is this Professor Fermi's residence?" On being assured that it was, she merely said: "I wish to inform you that this evening at six o'clock, Professor Fermi will receive a call from Stockholm."

That was all.

But Fermi knew immediately what the call meant. Stockholm, in Sweden, was where the world-famous Nobel Prizes were awarded, and it had been rumored that Enrico Fermi might win one for his research with neutrons. So the rumor must be true!

Now there would be no problem about leaving Italy. Mussolini would not forbid a Nobel Prize winner to go to Sweden, to accept his prize in person. Indeed, it would suit Mussolini very well to have an Italian stand up in Stockholm to show the whole world how clever Italian scientists were. Nor would he refuse to allow the man's family to be present at the ceremony.

So the Fermis started packing—to go to Sweden. But even as Fermi and his wife stood beside the telephone, they both knew that Stockholm would be only their first stop. They would not return to Rome. Instead they would join those thousands upon thousands of other people who had sailed across an ocean to seek freedom in America.

6

THE LAND OF LIBERTY

Salt spray rose in a mist as the ship plowed through the gray water. The sky was gray, too, early on this January morning in 1939. Enrico Fermi stood on the deck, staring ahead eagerly. Suddenly, he turned and hurried below to call his wife and children.

"Wake up and dress," he urged. "Hurry!"

Back on the deck, he pointed toward a ghostly shadow of darker gray looming up out of the mist. As they watched, it became clearer, and the jagged peaks of a giant city appeared.

"Land!" shouted Nella, who was going to be eight years old in a few weeks.

Plump little Giulio, who was almost three, clapped his hands.

Then off to one side, they saw another sight that, on this gray winter morning, had a very special meaning to them. The Statue of Liberty! For a few minutes, Fermi stood in silence, then a smile lit his face and he turned to his wife.

"We have founded the American branch of the Fermi family," he said.

In the months that followed, they found it was not so easy, though, to begin a new life in New York City. Even finding an apartment was hard. When they had left Rome, nobody was supposed to know they would not return, so they had not been able to take much money with them, or their furniture. Arriving in New York, they needed a place to live that would not cost too much, and was already furnished.

At Columbia University, where Fermi was to teach, he heard that a certain Mrs. Smith had an apartment for rent that might suit them. Mrs. Fermi went to look at it. She found the building without too much trouble, but then she had another problem.

"I want Mrs. Zmeeth," she told the elevator operator.

He shook his head.

"Mrs. *Zmeeth!*" she repeated.

Still he shook his head. "Nobody here by that name," he said.

At last, in desperation, Mrs. Fermi took a

46

"We have founded the American branch of the Fermi family."

scrap of paper out of her purse and wrote "Smith" on it. "Oh!" said the elevator man, and then promptly took her to the right floor. Fortunately, it was a nice apartment, with an impressive view of the Hudson River. Mrs. Fermi was glad to rent it, and avoid further house-hunting adventures.

Once settled, they still faced many problems. Mrs. Fermi worried about whether the children would ever be able to make friends, and about how Nella could possibly manage to learn in an American school.

Even the children's clothing set them apart from the American children they now met. Nella's winter coat and leggings had been hand-made, in the European style, and although the outfit was quite elegant, it seemed to startle Americans. People stopped on the street to gaze at her curiously.

Then there was the matter of getting along in school. In Italy, Nella had been in the third grade, but her new teachers wanted to see if she could do third-grade work in America. So they gave her some tests.

One question was: A little boy has taken a hike in the country, where he played with a small animal. Upon returning home he must wash thoroughly, and change his smelly clothes. What is the animal he played with?

But in Italy there were no skunks. Nella had never seen or heard of such an animal and could not answer the question. Nevertheless, she worked hard at her English—and, after all, she was put in the third grade.

With this problem more or less solved, the family still had all sorts of other difficulties. To Mrs. Fermi, even buying food was an adventure at first. Once she asked for butter, and the clerk handed her a box of bird seed! Then she discovered that many of the small markets in the area had at least one man behind the counter who had been born in Italy. By speaking Italian to them, she could buy what she wanted—and they also helped her with her English.

Meanwhile, Fermi himself was going through something of the same process at Columbia. Right at the outset, he made a sort of deal with one of his students. "I will teach you physics," Fermi said, "and you, please, will teach me English." Although Fermi could speak the language fairly well by now, after the several summers he had spent in America, he still had difficulty pronouncing certain words. Now he wanted to master English, even the slang he heard in the streets. He also wanted to find out all he possibly could about American customs.

The student he picked as his own professor was a promising young man named Herbert

Anderson. Soon the whole family was used to hearing at the dinner table what Anderson had taught his teacher that day.

"Anderson says 'to the tune of' doesn't always have anything to do with music," Fermi reported. "If the government is spending money to the tune of a million dollars, that just means it's spending a lot of money."

Then the next day: "Anderson says some students in America work their way through college by waiting on tables."

And next: "Anderson says we should hire our neighbor's children. Anderson says we should pay them a penny for each of our English mistakes they correct. Anderson says . . . Anderson says . . . Anderson says . . ." It got to be a big joke in the Fermi family.

At last, Anderson himself came to dinner. Instead of the owlish young man they had expected, he was friendly and unassuming. He was not awed by Fermi's great reputation, and simply wanted to be helpful. Then the whole family began to save up their questions about America for Anderson.

7

CP-1

Even while Fermi was busy learning, he was starting on a momentous path. Just two weeks after he arrived in New York, he went to meet a ship as it docked. On board was a friend of his, Professor Niels Bohr of Denmark, who brought him amazing news.

Bohr was the world's greatest expert on the structure of the atom, and he had come to visit America as a sort of ambassador. He came to report in person something he thought was of world-shaking importance.

More than four years ago in Rome, Fermi had bombarded uranium. When neutrons struck the uranium, it had seemed that a new element was formed. Then newspapers had hailed Fermi—and now Bohr had to tell him that he had been hailed *for the wrong reason!*

Bohr had come to tell Fermi and other leading physicists in the United States what it was that Fermi had really accomplished. And the truth was even more startling than what had been suspected. Only now was it evident that Fermi had *split* the uranium atom!

There could be no doubt anymore, because a team of German scientists had recently repeated the same experiments, and then gone a step farther. Having new methods at their disposal for studying complicated substances, they had been able to study the materials that the bombarding produced.

Then they were stunned to discover that *barium* was present, besides other elements close to uranium in weight. But barium was only about half as heavy as uranium. No previous bombarding experiments had ever produced an element so different from the original. Where could the barium have come from?

A woman physicist named Lise Meitner had suggested the answer. The bombarding must have caused the *fission,* or the breaking up, of some uranium atoms, she said. Then she did some complicated mathematics—and arrived at the world-shaking conclusion Bohr had come to report.

For the barium and other end products produced by the uranium fission were not quite as heavy as the original uranium had been. But it was a basic law of science that *matter can be neither created nor destroyed*. So the missing matter must have shot forth in the form of energy!

Fermi immediately grasped what this meant. The Einstein theory had said there were huge amounts of energy locked up in atoms, but until now it had been doubtful if man could ever get at this energy. Now it seemed that man might be on the way!

So far, the fission produced in laboratory experiments was on a very small scale. The energy released could not be detected easily, or made to serve man's purpose. Still, this was a start! And almost at once, Fermi thought of a possible next step.

Suppose it should turn out that when a uranium atom split, among the things that happened was the release of neutrons? Fermi asked Bohr the question, and Bohr nodded gravely. They both understood the implications of the question.

For if man could aim a neutron at uranium, and the neutron hit a uranium atom . . . and then the splitting atom released other neutrons—*other uranium atoms might split*. Then if these, in turn, released additional neutrons, still more uranium atoms might break up. A *chain reaction,* in which a large number of uranium atoms would split, would then take place.

Was such a chain reaction really possible? Suppose it was—and man could control it! That thought caused the grave looks Fermi and Bohr exchanged as they discussed the subject. Without any need to say the word aloud, they both knew that the explosive energy from such a chain reaction quite possibly could be used for a —*bomb!*

Now it seemed clear that the world was on the brink of a great war. Hitler had already seized Austria and Czechoslovakia; he was threatening Poland, which England and France had sworn to protect. Suppose Hitler should get his hands on an atomic bomb!

Nor did this seem too unlikely. Bohr had just told Fermi that talented German scientists were working on fission. The free world had no official means for mobilizing its scientists. So what was to be done?

Almost immediately, Fermi started on a new series of uranium experiments at Columbia. Another European-born physicist, Leo Szilard of Hungary, joined him. And within months, it began to look as if these two refugees, who had fled to America in search of freedom, might be on the right track. It seemed they *might* be able to give their new land a big lead in atomic research.

But they would need money for pure uranium —"money to the tune of millions of dollars," Fermi told Anderson, who was working with him. Furthermore, it seemed important that the President of the United States should know what it was that they might accomplish.

Thus just a month before Hitler marched on Poland and started the Second World War, Szilard drove down to Princeton, New Jersey. Albert Einstein, the most famous living scientist, was there. Being Jewish, he had fled Germany a few years earlier. Szilard thought Einstein was the best man to tell President Roosevelt about the possibilities of atomic power. Einstein did so, in this historic letter:

August 2, 1939

F.D. Roosevelt,
President of the United States
White House
Washington, D.C.

Sir:

Some recent work by E. Fermi and L. Szilard . . . leads me to expect that the element uranium may be turned into a new and important source of energy in the near future. . . .

Einstein told the President it appeared almost

certain that a way to wrest vast amounts of power from uranium *"could be achieved in the immediate future."* He also said it was conceivable—but less likely—that *"extremely powerful bombs of a new type may thus be constructed."*

Then Einstein warned that new and secret atomic research was already going on in Germany. And he suggested that giving official support for similar research might well be investigated by the United States. On receiving the letter, President Roosevelt did appoint a committee to do this.

Meanwhile, Fermi worked away at Columbia. First he proved that uranium atoms *did* release neutrons as they split, and so a chain reaction *was* possible. Then he had to solve what seemed an almost endless series of problems before arriving at a way to create—and control—an *atomic pile*.

This actually was a pile of blocks, like bricks. For he decided to use graphite, the same black substance that is the "lead" in lead pencils, to slow down neutrons. Wedged in among blocks of solid graphite would be lumps of uranium. By the most intricate of calculations, he was able to conclude that when a pile reached a certain size and shape, a chain reaction would probably occur.

But it took him many months of hard and

dirty work to arrive at this conclusion. While part of the work was purely mental, he found it necessary to check his calculations along the way by building and testing a greasy, dusty wall of graphite.

By the time Fermi was all but certain that he knew how a pile should be built, the United States itself was at war. The Japanese bombed Pearl Harbor, and we were fighting in Europe and the Pacific. As the result of Einstein's letter and the war emergency, a new and super-secret agency of the government had been established to take over atomic research. Besides Fermi, there were other research teams working on the chain reaction problem at other universities. Early in 1942, it was decided that they should all work together—in Chicago. What they began to build together was CP-1.

To those very few in the know, this stood for Chicago Pile No. 1. But by now, even Mrs. Fermi had no idea about what her husband was doing, for the strictest secrecy had been imposed. All she could be told when they had to pick up and move to Chicago was that her husband was now working for something called "the Metallurgical Laboratory."

Absolutely the only information given out about this mysterious laboratory was the bare fact that some sort of research involving metals was being carried forward. Even the location of the lab was not to be discussed—and a strange location it was.

To build a pile of the size Fermi wanted, a very large room was needed. He chose a squash court under the rising rows of seats at the University of Chicago's football stadium. Even before the war emergency, this serious-minded school had given up football; now the peculiar old stadium, that looked on the outside like a medieval castle, began serving a serious purpose indeed.

For several months, a crew of strong young physics students cut pure, black graphite into bricks. Then they arranged the bricks in a big, squarish mass that rose higher and higher. The work went on around the clock, directed with much care by Fermi himself, his manner friendly but business-like. *He* seemed completely confident.

On the morning of December 2, 1942, Fermi announced that the pile had reached the right size. There were certain control rods imbedded in it; when these were withdrawn, he said, the chain reaction would start.

But could it be stopped once it started? A "suicide squad" was poised on a ladder, just to make sure. They had a liquid with them, that should make the pile stop if other controls failed. Yet nobody, not even Fermi, could say positively

At nine forty-five that morning, Fermi ordered that the first of the control rods be withdrawn.

what was going to happen. When he gave the signal, for the first time in human history man was going to try to set off a nuclear chain reaction.

At nine forty-five that morning, Fermi ordered that the first of the control rods be withdrawn. A switch was thrown. A small motor whined. Beside him, on the balcony where he stood, were special instruments to detect neutron activity. These began to click faster, and a pen traced a rising line.

"The line will level off soon," Fermi said quietly. And it did.

Then he ordered another control removed, and again the instruments showed what was happening. The graph pen moved upward again. The clicking increased in speed—and leveled off again.

The last of the control rods was known as "Zip." This was to be pulled out slowly, a foot at a time.

"Zip out to thirteen feet," Fermi now ordered. They all waited, scarcely breathing. The graph pen moved higher. The clicking got faster. "But this is still not it," Fermi said. "It will level off." And it did.

Then "Zip" was moved to twelve feet, eleven, ten. "But this is still not it," Fermi said each time. With each passing minute, the tension mounted.

Suddenly, Fermi smiled. "I'm hungry," he said. "Let's go to lunch."

After lunch, the test was resumed, and finally, at twenty-five minutes past three, Fermi turned to Dr. Arthur Compton, who was in general charge of several secret research projects. "This will do it," he said. "Now the pen will climb, and continue to climb. It will not level off."

He gave the order to remove the control rod one foot more, and the pen began to climb again. *It did not level off!*

For twenty-eight minutes, every eye watched tensely while the graph pen kept rising higher—and then Fermi nodded. "Okay," he said. "Zip in!"

The control rod jammed back into the pile. Instantly the clicking slowed! The pen slid downhill! *CP-1 had chain-reacted—and then been stopped!*

Now one of the watching physicists held out the bottle of wine he had kept behind his back for hours, and paper cups were brought. Solemnly, all who were present drank to a new era —*the atomic era.*

A few minutes later, Arthur Compton went to a telephone to report to Washington, in his own code.

"The Italian navigator has landed in the New World!" he said.

8

SITE Y

The United States Army had a lot of confidence in Enrico Fermi. Even before the historic test of CP-1, a general had spent millions of dollars gambling that the test would work.

He was Brigadier General Leslie R. Groves, the commander of an Army unit with an innocent name—the Manhattan District Project. What General Groves was really in charge of could not be told at the time. His actual mission was to get an atomic bomb built.

Toward this end, General Groves went on a land-buying spree during 1942. He bought tens of thousands of acres of land in three different states—Tennessee, New Mexico and Washington. After the success of the Chicago test, Fermi went to "Site Y" in New Mexico.

A few months earlier, there had been a small private school for boys on this high and lonely mesa near Los Alamos Canyon. Then along came General Groves to say the school must close down. For the Army wanted complete privacy there from then on.

Almost overnight, rows of apartments were built. Laboratories, a few stores, even a grade school sprang up. Then all over the country, noted scientists and their families began to "disappear." Nobody knew where they had gone—except General Groves and a very small number of other high officials.

The air was sparkling clear up on the mesa, but only those special people with special passes could turn off the highway below, and take the narrow, winding road that led to the secret town. Tourists definitely were not welcome. Barbed wire fences surrounded the whole area.

Inside the fences, people spoke of the new town as Los Alamos. But this was a name that had yet to appear on a map. Indeed, Los Alamos was extraordinary in many respects. General Groves mentioned one of these in a speech he made to some of his Army officers.

"At great expense," he said, "we have gathered on this mesa the largest collection of crackpots ever seen!"

But he smiled as he said it, because the general was fond of his "crackpots." Even if some of them acted a trifle absent-mindedly, or talked with thick accents, he had great faith in their ability.

He was counting on these scientists, who came from many countries, to design and construct the world's first atomic bomb. That was the task set for Site Y. Meanwhile, at Site X in Tennessee —later known as Oak Ridge—uranium was being purified. The third secret city, Hanford in the state of Washington, was to make *plutonium*. This was a brand new element produced when uranium chain-reacted; plutonium would probably be the substance used for the bomb itself.

Fermi went out to Hanford first, when he left Chicago—because he had been summoned to solve a baffling problem there, before settling down at Los Alamos. Now he was considered such a valuable individual that he was not allowed to risk flying, and he had to take a train instead.

But it was hard for him to sit still more than a few hours at a time. Fortunately, the fellow physicist who was traveling with him had a bright idea when Fermi got restless. "You know, Enrico," he said, "when I was mountain climbing last summer, I noticed my watch was affected. It wasn't accurate at high altitudes. Can you explain that?"

Fermi whipped out his pocket slide rule at once. Delighted to have a new problem to challenge his mind, he went right to work calculating the effect of thinner mountain air on a watch's mechanism.

By the time he had solved the much more complicated problems plaguing Hanford, and then arrived at Los Alamos, his family was already there. Mrs. Fermi had traveled out with the children—under an assumed name. Lest anyone be curious about why the wife of a famous physicist was going to New Mexico, she had done as she was told and bought her tickets as *Mrs. Eugene Farmer.*

On stepping down from the train at Santa Fé, she was relieved to see a young soldier, obviously waiting to meet her and the children. She had been promised that someone would be there, to take them wherever it was they were going, yet she had not been able to help worrying. Suppose they were forgotten! What would she do? Because she was so flustered, she did the wrong thing when the soldier walked up to her and said:

"Are you Mrs. *Farmer?*"

"Yes, I am Mrs. *Fermi,*" she said.

"I was told to call you Mrs. Farmer," he said, and looked at her sternly, as if she had given away an important military secret.

Happily, she had not done any great harm, but the incident was a good preparation for life at Los Alamos. Even the children had to carry identity cards all the time; nobody could go through the gates without the proper card.

But the Fermi children thoroughly enjoyed this new and odd existence. It was like playing spy all day long. With the other children who lived there, they made a game after school of creeping around the barbed wire fences. Whenever they drove through the gates, they always ducked down to try to fool the sentries.

Yet they had not the slightest idea about the reason for all the secrecy. Their father never spoke a word about what it was he did in his laboratory, nor did any of the men ever talk about their work. None of the wives and children knew why they were living in this mystery town. Even during gay family picnics in the surrounding hills, or ski trips in the winter, the subject was never discussed.

Only one small hint was given to Mrs. Fermi. A tall, aging man suddenly appeared at Los Alamos, and he was supposed to be called Mr. Nicholas Baker. But Mrs. Fermi knew better. He was Professor Niels Bohr, who had escaped from Denmark after Hitler had conquered it.

Bohr was so widely known as an atomic expert that, even in the closely-guarded Los Alamos, his name could not be spoken aloud—lest some-one hear it, and conclude an atomic research project was underway.

Although Mrs. Fermi recognized him, she did not let herself ask any questions. Nor did any of the women. They were so well trained that they did not even ask questions when virtually all of the men at Los Alamos disappeared early in July of 1945.

By that time, Germany had surrendered and the war in Europe was over. But Japan was yet to be beaten, which might take years of hard fighting, the newspapers warned. The newspapers did not know about Los Alamos, let alone about the reason why the men working there were suddenly leaving.

Only afterwards did it become known that Fermi and the others had departed to go deep into the desert of southern New Mexico. As far away from people as possible, they were ready to arrange one of the most awesome experiments in all human history. *They had built an atomic bomb—and now the time had come to test it!*

On the morning of July 16, 1945, Enrico Fermi stood with the rest of the official observers, about ten miles from the bomb site. Perhaps more than any other single man, he had made this test possible. Now he had no doubt that it would succeed.

He was busy dropping scraps of paper down toward the ground!

"Minus twenty minutes!" called the countdown relay. Scientists and Army men waited, some of them fearful, all of them silent.

"Minus fifteen!" The watchers put on special, very dark glasses, to protect their eyes.

"Minus ten!"

"Minus five!"

"*Now!*"

A weird light glared out, gold and purple. Then came a roar. And a cloud like a giant mushroom rose up in the air, above the *first atomic explosion* ever set off by man. But Fermi neither saw nor heard any of this, he later told his wife, because he was too busy.

He was busy dropping scraps of paper down toward the ground!

There was method in this seeming madness. Fermi was measuring the power of the blast by his own simple system. He dropped his scraps, and then watched; the air was so stirred up by the explosion that the bits of paper were dragged some distance. Fermi paced off the distance, and took out his slide rule.

The figure he arrived at came astonishingly close to the figure that complicated instruments later provided.

Even after the test, Fermi could not tell his wife about it. Now the scientists had done their part, but the bomb was still a top secret—for another few weeks.

Then President Harry Truman arrived at a decision. It would shorten the war, and save many lives in the long run, if the United States dropped an atomic bomb on Japan. On the morning of August 6, Hiroshima was hit; two days later, Nagasaki was the target.

After that, Japan surrendered.

9

PEACE!

"The war is over! THE WAR IS OVER!"

It was August 14, 1945. In every street of Los Alamos, there were radios blaring, and children shouting. Then some of the boys grabbed up pots and spoons and ran out, banging away. A parade formed, a wonderfully happy, laughing, dancing parade.

To the children of Los Alamos, it seemed they had a special reason to celebrate. For a week, big headlines in the newspapers had been telling what *their* fathers had accomplished. Now, because of their fathers, the terrible war had ended.

But some of these fathers wore serious looks. During long months, they had done their best to solve complicated scientific problems, and they had succeeded. They had learned how to tap the energy of the atom. By their efforts, they had brought the dawn of a new age—the atomic age.

Yet at the same time, they had also made it possible to kill millions of people. In Hiroshima and in Nagasaki, tens of thousands had died already. The full horror of what had happened in those two cities would not be known for months, or years; people would keep on dying, from the dangerous rays the bombs had released.

Was science evil to give man such a weapon?

The question tormented some of those same scientists who had worked as hard as they could at Los Alamos to build the first bomb. But not Enrico Fermi.

"It does no good to try to keep knowledge from going forward," Fermi told his wife gravely. "Suppose we had decided to stop our work, and destroyed all our data. Others would be bound to rediscover whatever we had destroyed. Then in whose hands would the atomic bomb be placed?"

Many agreed with Fermi that the world would have been far worse off if Germany had beaten the United States in the race to build an atomic bomb. They also agreed that scientists loyal to the United States had had no choice: it was their duty to work on the bomb project.

But once the United States had built a stock of bombs, *should it have used them?*

This was the big question now—at Los Alamos and all over the world. Everywhere, men debated and debated about whether President Truman had made the right decision. "Mass murder!" some people protested. "In the long run, he saved many lives," others said.

Nowhere was the debate more vigorous than at Los Alamos itself. "For such a long time, we could not talk at all about our work," Fermi commented to his wife wryly. "Now it seems as if we can talk about nothing else."

He thought that in a way it was only natural for the scientists not to have worried much about the bomb while they were working on it. Down through the years, other people had always teased scientists about living in "an ivory tower." And it was true, Fermi thought, that science had to be studied somewhat away from the distractions of everyday life, in the sort of imaginary shelter that other people called an ivory tower. Up on their lonely mesa, far removed from the war itself, no wonder the scientists had failed to imagine Hiroshima.

Yet Fermi did not agree with his fellow physicists who now accused themselves of failing mankind. "We should have protested!" these men insisted. "We knew what the bomb could do. We should have stopped Truman!" To this, Fermi gravely shook his head.

Nor would he join in when many of the men at Los Alamos formed a new committee. Their goal was to make sure that no more atomic bombs would ever be dropped. They wanted to see the United Nations, or some other international body, take control of nuclear research. Then, they believed, the power of the atom would be used for peaceful purposes only—not war.

Fermi could not go along with them because he thought these were matters for statesmen, and not scientists, to decide. As a citizen, he hoped a way could be found to avoid war in the future; as a scientist, he wanted to concentrate on science, instead of moving out of his laboratory to become a special pleader for any cause.

Indeed, he could hardly wait to start work again on various of his own ideas. Even before the war was over, he and some of his friends at Los Alamos had been talking about a plan. Several of them were specialists in different areas. but they decided to join forces.

It had been a rewarding experience for them all, working together as a team at Los Alamos. Now they wanted to carry this same team spirit over into peacetime research—and the University of Chicago was anxious to have them.

So on the last day of 1945, the Fermi family

Then on the lapel of Fermi's jacket, General Groves pinned a medal, the Congressional Medal of Merit, the nation's highest civilian honor.

packed up again, to move back to Chicago.

In a way, Fermi was sorry to leave Los Alamos. Living and working there had been a rare kind of pleasure. Apart from the excitement of the work itself, it had been exciting getting to know so many talented scientists so well. On top of their mesa, with nobody else for miles around, they had sat up late together many an evening, enjoying the sparks flying from so many keen minds. And the bright New Mexico sunshine, the golden mountains in the distance, were so beautiful. Yes, Fermi would miss Los Alamos. But the story of his stay there was not finished yet.

A few months after he left, the man who had sent him there in the first place paid him a visit in Chicago. General Groves brought along proof that Los Alamos, for its part, had appreciated Fermi. On behalf of the President of the United States, the general made a little speech:

"Dr. Enrico Fermi . . . the first man in all the world to achieve nuclear chain reaction . . . Associate Director of the Los Alamos Laboratory . . . his sound scientific judgment, his initiative and resourcefulness and his unswerving devotion to duty have contributed vitally . . . ."

Then on the lapel of Fermi's jacket, General Groves pinned a medal, the Congressional Medal of Merit, the nation's highest civilian honor.

10

A LAST TOY

In 1946, Fermi was forty-five years old—a little old for a physicist, he would laughingly say. But his mind showed no signs of slowing down. It seemed full as ever with new research ideas.

Indeed, his fellow physicists coined a new word that indicated how very unusual they thought Enrico Fermi was. In the language of science, *micro-* means *one-millionth of;* a micro-volt, for instance, is one-millionth of a volt. The new word was *micro-Fermi,* and it was used this way:

"Have you heard what young Dr. C_____ has been doing?" one physicist might ask another.

"Oh, I wouldn't pay too much attention to what he's doing," the other might answer. "You know, he's a *micro-Fermi!*"

If Fermi knew his name was being used like this, as a short-cut to measure other minds, he probably was amused. Just as in his younger days, he still had a most disarming manner when it came to his own mental prowess. He was not conceited, but not exactly modest either.

The same Anderson who had been one of his first American students was still working with him. Now they were both valued staff members at the University of Chicago's new Institute for Nuclear Studies. Fermi liked Anderson tremendously—but a fact was a fact.

"Do you know," Fermi said to Anderson one morning, "it's simply amazing." He had just returned from a brief visit to Los Alamos, where he spent some time with John Von Neumann, the great mathematician. "Von Neumann's mind is as much faster than mine," said Fermi to Anderson, *"as mine is than yours."*

Nevertheless, any student who had a scientific idea he wanted to talk about could be sure of at least a few minutes of Fermi's valuable time. Professor Fermi might not have time for his family, his wife teasingly complained, but he always had time for science.

True, he did snatch odd minutes every day to

read newspapers, and almost every evening he had an hour for one of the adventure stories he enjoyed so much. Captain Horatio Hornblower, a brave sailor in a whole series of books, was his favorite hero. And Fermi still craved exercise, so the family went skiing, or on long walks in the country.

Nevertheless, the largest portion by far of his time and energy went to his work. If Mrs. Fermi had thought he would relax once the war was over, she was mistaken. For now the University of Chicago was building him a great new toy— and every detail about it was endlessly fascinating to him.

The "toy" was a giant *cyclotron*. This was a piece of scientific equipment that had not even existed when he was working in Rome. Basically, a cyclotron was a big magnet encased in a box. With it, very strong currents of electricity could be used for experimental purposes.

Even the earliest cyclotrons, back in the late 1930's, had been of immense value. At Columbia, Fermi had first used a cyclotron to supply neutrons for his tests with uranium. Professor Ernest O. Lawrence of California had won a Nobel Prize for building the first cyclotron; and at the University of California, the machine had been used to produce the world's first plutonium.

Now far more powerful cyclotrons were being

built. In California, Lawrence had a new giant buried under a remote hillside, to make sure no dangerous rays escaped. But in Chicago, Fermi was getting his toy right close at hand, in a pit under the new research building on the university campus. This was directly across the street from the stadium where the famous squash court had been. (Because the old stone walls of the court might have been contaminated by radiation, it had been torn down; but a small, square sign marked the spot where it had stood, and every day sightseeing buses stopped so that tourists could take pictures of it.)

Fermi was getting his cyclotron in such a handy location—"because we're lazy," he joked. But, of course, it was perfectly safe. By burying it so deep, he and his co-workers made sure there was no danger at all.

The special magnet constructed for their cyclotron weighed more than two thousand *tons*. This was almost forty times as heavy as the magnet in Lawrence's first machine. Because it was so enormous, it had to be delivered in sections, on trailer-trucks especially designed for such great weight. Policemen stood watching as these were unloaded, in case the pavement cracked and the street had to be closed.

This gigantic magnet was imbedded in a metal box big enough to store three hundred

The ''toy'' was a giant *cyclotron.*

bushels of grain. But nothing was stored in it, except the magnet itself—not even air. Nine pumps kept it a perfect vacuum.

Within this airless chamber, invisible and almost unbelievably tiny particles could be whirled around until they reached enormous speed. To scientists, a cyclotron was an *accelerator:* this means it could accelerate, or speed up, electrically-charged particles. Such particles from the nucleus, or inner core, of atoms, would ordinarily fly off in a straight line. But in a cyclotron, the magnet bent their path, so they traveled around and around, faster and faster. And physicists could try all sorts of tests, to study the atom.

For even if man had learned to tap atomic energy, the atom still held many secrets. Already, radioactive elements were being used—in medicine, to treat cancer; in agriculture, to grow new plants; in industry, to develop new products. Nuclear submarines were being planned, as were nuclear powerhouses, to turn on the lights in areas where coal or other conventional fuels could not be obtained easily. But the cost of such projects was very high. Perhaps more research would uncover better ways for releasing the energy of atoms. Indeed, countless facts still remained to be discovered. With his great new toy, Fermi hoped to add still more to man's store of knowledge.

Almost as if he suspected that his time was

growing short, he worked all day and often at night, too, after the Chicago cyclotron was finished in 1951. He was studying new particles that were still a mystery, and starting to work out new theories that would explain their behavior.

Then in the spring of 1954, Fermi for the first time in his life felt unwell. He was tired, even when he got up in the morning, and he let Mrs. Fermi convince him to see a doctor. But the doctor could not find the trouble.

Then, although he felt no better, Fermi insisted on going ahead with a planned trip. He went back to his native Italy as the guest of honor at a special summer school. He lectured brilliantly, people said; somehow he even summoned up the strength to climb a mountain.

But when he returned to Chicago, he felt so ill that there was no longer any question about it. He had to go to a hospital. There doctors found he had developed a rare form of cancer which could not be cured.

After the doctors told him this, Fermi went home, still making plans. "I really ought to write a physics text," he said to his wife. On the days he felt well, he asked for his notebooks. But the disease traveled fast. At home on Sunday morning, November 30, 1954, at the age of fifty-three, he died peacefully in his sleep.

The world of science marked its loss in many

ways. At the University of Chicago, the research unit Fermi had helped to found was given a new name. It became the Enrico Fermi Institute for Nuclear Studies. The United States Atomic Energy Commission named its annual award for outstanding scientific achievement the Enrico Fermi Prize.

And many men who had worked with Fermi spoke out about the debt they had owed him. Often, they said, it was he who had suggested some new line they should take; it was he who deserved credit for what they had done.

No other scientist in this century had mastered the whole field of physics as Fermi had, they said. He had reached the highest summits, both in theory and experiment. Nor did it seem likely, as physics kept on growing more complex, that any man would ever again be able to dominate it as Fermi had.

"Enrico Fermi," they said, "was *exceptional!*"